BEYOND TO NEW LIFE

Unleashing the power within each of us

Sister Judy Blake, CSJ

Dedication

In gratitude to God who called us to this ministry, to our Adrian Dominican and Congregation of St. Joseph communities who sustain us in our ministry, for our many volunteers who chose to serve the poor with us as well as our families, friends, sponsors and donors we couldn't have made it this far without you. Finally, to our board members and the many women who trusted the process to better their lives.

To learn more about the N.E.W. Life Center, please visit
our website at http://stlukenewlifecenter.com/.

Table of Contents

Introduction

When you belong to a religious congregation such as the Sisters of St. Joseph or the Adrian Dominicans you are required by canon law to do an annual retreat. It is a gift we are given to recharge our ministry batteries through prayer, meditation, and silence. Usually it is an eight-day retreat but once in a lifetime it can be a 30-day retreat. It is a glorious opportunity to step out of ministry and leave the world and all its chaos behind.

In June of 1991 my request for a 30-day retreat was granted. The timing was perfect, because in August I was beginning a new ministry at St. Agnes parish in Flint, MI. This retreat would help me clear my mind, rest my body, and open my heart for work that lay ahead of me. Eagerly I packed my car and headed to Sedalia Colorado to Sacred Heart Jesuit Retreat House. It is nestled in the foothills of the mountains, with cattle roaming the open range around the retreat house. It rains a little bit each day just enough to create a beautiful rainbow.

The environment, the liturgies, the daily meetings with the retreat director contributed to the perfect experience for me. I really wasn't expecting any outcome for this retreat. I just wanted to be open to God and any blessings that would come my way. The one blessing I received was a peace I never experienced before. It was a joy to be there. Then an unexpected event began - a dream - not just one night but frequently repeated during the last half of my retreat.

The dream was the same each time I had it. There were people whose faces were not clearly seen and they were all saying to me, "Help us; we're gifted; we can do things; we just need someone to help us."

I shared this series of dreams with my director and she said, "You need to seriously pray about this. God is definitely trying to tell you something important." I did but by the end of the retreat I was still in the dark about its meaning.

Upon my return home I shared this experience with my friend, Sr. Carol; her response was, "You really need to pray about this; God has a message in it for you." In view of the new ministry ahead of me I put it on the back burner - actually for several years even though it continued to reoccur.

In 1994, after three years of ministry at St. Agnes, I moved 1.8 miles southwest to St. Luke. I was installed as Pastoral Coordinator by Bishop Povish.

A pastoral coordinator is responsible for all the roles of a priest pastor except administering sacraments and presiding at liturgy. A priest is assigned to the parish as the sacramental minister.

We all know that hindsight is 20/20. Looking back I understand this was the place where God would play that trump card; the retreat dream would begin to be revealed. This Sister of St. Joseph would go where she could never have conceived of going.

Chapter One
The Beginning

Sr. Carol Weber is an Adrian Dominican Sister whom I met in 1984 at St. John the Baptist parish in Ypsilanti, MI. I was just hired to be the outreach coordinator. We became friends during my five years of ministry there. It was the beginning of lifelong friendship.

Sr. Carol served for six years as the Director of Formation for the Adrian Dominican Sisters. This ministry took her to their formation house in the Dominican Republic (DR) several times. While she was there, she was moved by the ministry of the sisters who invited the neighborhood women to a prayer and sharing experience. The faith of the women deepened and their self-esteem grew significantly, because they began to understand they were beloved by God.

After formation Sr. Carol was appointed Pastoral Coordinator at St. Francis of Assisi parish in Otisville, MI. We decided to live in community together. During our time as coordinators Sr. Carol and I decided to get a doctorate degree through the Ecumenical Theological Seminary in Detroit, MI. We both received Doctor of Ministry degrees.

During doctoral studies Sr. Carol changed ministries working part time at Sts. Charles and Helena Parish in Clio, MI. It was there that the desire and call became clear to begin the ministry to women that was modeled in the DR. Her dream was pulling her to the materially poor women in Flint, MI. Compelled by her dream Sr. Carol came to St. Luke parish, first at part time and shortly thereafter full time.

Needless to say, that after all these transitions, Sr. Carol never gave up on asking, "When are you going to do something about that dream?" My excuse was that I was too busy. I felt I was but evidently God saw things differently. God has a great sense of humor and was not going let the dream go unfinished.

One year, Sr. Carol was the sponsor for her niece, Alison, for confirmation. One Sunday each month during her preparation, Sr. Carol attended classes with Alison. After class early in November Sr. Carol came home on a mission! She walked and sat down on her chair not even taking off her coat. "Oh! Oh!" crossed my mind. "Hi, how'd it go today?" I asked. A huge God administered trump card falls. "You've got to do something about that dream of yours," Sr. Carol said commandingly. "Okay, what's up?" I countered. "Well," she said, "Alison and I have to do a service project before confirmation and I thought it was time you did something about that dream of yours." I knew it! She was contemplating this all the way home. "Okay, so when is this project due?" "In two weeks." "Impossible! Two weeks? It can't be done!" "And why not? Can't we do a clothes drive and take them out on the street to the homeless? How hard can that be?" All said in voice command, "We're doing it and that's that!"

The following Sunday I announced the project to the parish asking for donations of warm clothing and blankets to take to the homeless. I also thought it a good idea to invite our confirmation students to join us for their projects. One mom responded positively. Jennifer and two of her children could help.

Clothes came in that week, enough to fill two mini-vans. The next hurdle was about where to find the homeless. Someone told me to go to railroad tracks. Railroad tracks? Flint is home to Buick City, Chevy Truck and Bus, Metal Fab, and an Engine plant. There are probably a hundred miles of track weaving in, out, and around Flint. We decided the most logical place would be the North End Soup Kitchen.

Twelve days after the "grand announcement" Alison came to our house on Friday night so she and Aunt Carol could bake cookies to take to the soup kitchen.

They made chocolate chip and peanut butter cookies (peanut butter because of its protein). "There's not enough peanut butter for them to qualify as a health food," said I. They ignored me and continued baking.

Before Alison came she had made fleece scarves in wide variety of colors and patterns. On Saturday morning we packed a van with the cookies and scarves and some clothes Alison brought with her. We met Jennifer at St. Luke, loaded the three vans and headed toward the Soup Kitchen just a couple of miles away. The plan was to distribute the items from the tailgate of the vans. John Mance, the director of the soup kitchen, came out to the vans and asked what we were doing. We told him and since it was November and cold, he invited us to come inside.

We were certainly a welcome novelty for his clients. Three adult women and three young teens handing out badly needed winter clothes, homemade scarves and cookies. Our conversations with the homeless helped us understand their needs for clothing they can layer, warm socks and clean underwear. The huge thing for them was caring youth listening to their stories.

Of course the cookies were a big hit as were the scarves. The recipients staged a mini fashion show as they compared their new "outfits" with each other. But back to the cookies I previously criticized, one man approached Sr. Carol and asked, "Do you know these are homemade cookies?" "Yes, I do," she said. "Do you know how long it's been since I had a homemade cookie?" "No, I don't." He looked it over carefully and said, "Forty-one years." A small tear trickled down the side of his face.

Chapter Two
One Thing Leads to Another

When you say "Yes" to God things have a way of revving up. How can one simple service project to help three preteens understand that serving others is a good thing and then becomes a life-changing shake up for three adults?

We returned to the parish and unloaded a few left over items. I was thanking everyone when Jennifer said, "Sister Judy, this can't end here today. We really need to keep this ongoing." "She who suggests..." Her immediate response was, "My family and I will be there." So I recommended that after communion on Sunday we all share our experiences with the parish. The stories touched our community and the St. Luke Street Ministry was born. That afternoon on the 14th day of their project, Sr. Carol and Alison completed the confirmation assignment.

I had a sense that this wasn't going to be a one-time event. It took on a life of its own very quickly. People from parishes all over the diocese got wind of this new ministry and wanted to help. Families and confirmation groups joined us, university and college students, too. One Saturday per month we hit the streets with tables and chairs, clothes and blankets, socks and underwear and a hot dog lunch. We set up what looked like a giant flea market. Donations were so plentiful that we had a caravan of 10 to 26 cars and trucks loaded with give-a-ways.

We needed more sites around the city. A parishioner at St. Luke suggested we get in touch with Geneva Spears of the Soul Winning Jubilee. They were a group of prayer warriors hoping to win souls for Christ. For several years she took us to the urgently needy areas of Flint. We supplied the basic human needs and the group prayed for us and for the people who sought our help.

We listened to the stories of the men and women who came for help. One Saturday a woman pushing a grocery cart stopped at our tables. She and her children were living in an abandoned home. She was carrying her two-year old son and explained his medical problem; doctors told her he would never walk. One of our volunteers helped her find what she needed. Another got her and her son something to eat and drink. We gathered to listen to the music of the Geneva Spears of the Soul Winning Jubilee.

The prayer warriors surrounded the lady and her son. They prayed for a long time over them - a lot longer than usual. As I watched, the lead singer started to sway to the rhythm of the song. I briefly turned back to the tables when all of a sudden a huge commotion erupted near the mother and her child. One of our workers came running that a miracle had just happened. The child slipped off his mother's lap and was moving to the music. Prayers of praise, thanksgiving and awe were lifted up by the crowd. The mother and child walked home. All of us stood in wonderment, overwhelmed by what had happened.

On the following Sunday at church the miraculous event was related to the parish. Some believed and were moved; a few doubted; one questioned it. Another flat out said it was a hoax. My response was that God still works miracles even though we often miss them. This was one we noticed.

Chapter Three
God Is Definitely Up to Something

We knew we were meeting needs. So did our volunteers. We did some theological reflection after each experience on the streets. Sr. Carol and I reviewed the stories we heard and realized they were getting more and more critical. We met a woman we will call Mary. She was panhandling on a main street in Flint when she found us. She was crying, more like sobbing, so Sr. Carol and I sat down on the curb with her. We calmed her down so we could understand what she was trying to tell us.

Mary has ten children and a husband who was ill and lost a leg because of uncontrollable diabetes and high blood pressure. They were victims of a fire in which they lost everything. No agency was willing to help them. She had found a landlord who had a small house that was empty. She begged him to let them stay there until her husband's disability checks were resumed. Then they would pay him. Moved by her story he allowed them to move in.

Of the ten children the two youngest have medical issues. One is on a heart monitor and the other needs a nebulizer. There was no furniture in the house. The doctor told her the baby's health could be seriously compromised if he continued to sleep on the floor. There was no stove or refrigerator in the house. Mary found a hot plate on which she cooked for all twelve of them.

The kicker for this story is that she had just been diagnosed with advanced uterine cancer and needed to start treatment immediately. Mary told us she was not able to do that because her husband was soon to be a paraplegic - the other leg had to be removed. She needed to be his caregiver.

Sr. Carol and I quickly saw she required major help. Sr. Carol took four men with two trucks back to the parish. We had a donation earlier in the week of a stove and refrigerator. We also had furniture and a crib donated. There were beds and bedding and a bundle of food from our food pantry. While they were loading the items on their trucks and in Sister's van we helped her find clothes for everyone in the family.

When the trucks arrived from the church, we told her the contents were for her. First she stared in disbelief, cried some more and began singing that she met God today. Sr. Carol sang all the way home.

Arriving at her residence the volunteers were greeted by a bunch of children who stood amazed. Mary had the children help empty the vehicles. Our men set up the stove and refrigerator making sure the appliances worked. The kids were really excited when Sr. Carol brought them things to do, books, games, puzzles, coloring books and crayons.

This encounter happened in November. Is there a pattern here? The community was once again moved by the story. More people wanted to be involved. Volunteers from other parishes brought more volunteers. There was a real concern about the well-being of this family.

In December we decided to make their Christmas the best ever. We put together gifts for each child of clothes and toys. There were gifts for mom and dad, too. All the components for a Christmas dinner and enough for the following week were packed in the van. When we arrived at their house Sr. Carol went to the door and was greeted by the 14-year old son. This already mature teen who learned from his difficult life told her that we had already done more than enough for the family and he requested we give it to a family that needed it more than they. He even directed us to a family down the block that was struggling. He assured us that they were secure and doing fine.

Wow! We were blown away. So we went to the family he indicated and found a mom with ten kids about the same ages, sizes and gender as Mary's children. Tears of gratitude flowed as her children excitedly emptied the van.

Mary certainly gave her children strong values. We happen to cross paths with her husband when we were having a special give-a-way at Civic Park School. It was only a few blocks from St. Luke. The kids at that school were very poor and in need of clothes and shoes so we held a street ministry day for them. Mary's husband told us that she had died of cancer but he and the children were doing well. The generous son was college bound.

We seldom have follow-up with clients we service. It was nice to know this family was doing well. I'm sure Mary still watches over her family from heaven.

Chapter Four
Hey, Don't Push!

You know when God has a plan there is no getting around it. You will co-operate one way or another.

On a cold January Saturday we set up our wares as usual. We had a steaming pot of hot chili waiting for the people to come. It wasn't a long wait. Word got around that we had winter clothes and blankets.

At one point a woman (we will call her June) approached Sr. Carol and asked if she had newborn baby clothes. We usually kept baby clothes in a tote until people asked for them. Sr. Carol got the tote for her and kneeling in a snow bank they began searching for gender specific attire. June told her the clothes were not for her but for a woman who gave birth by herself in the abandoned house next to her the night before. She had no clue that someone was living there. When the woman gathered enough strength she got the neighbor's attention. June called 911 and the ambulance took mother and child to Hurley Hospital.

June went to the hospital with the women and her baby and was assured mother and child were fine. They could leave the hospital but they needed a car seat and clothes for the baby.

Two weeks earlier we had received a car seat in a donation. At the time Sr. Carol asked, "What are we going to do with this? The people we serve don't even have cars." Being a pack rat, I said, "I think we should keep it. Who knows, someone may come along who really needs it." Reluctantly Sr. Carol agreed to keep it. Ahem, that's one for the pack rat!

Sr. Carol went back to the parish, got the car seat and put a nice selection of clothing in it. We put June on the bus and paid her fare. We're sure she was a very welcome sight to that mom.

This turned out to be the proverbial "straw" that broke into an epiphany that opened the door for Sr. Carol's dream to come alive. On the way home from this street ministry we said simultaneously that we had to do more for the displaced and downtrodden women in Flint. We could no longer just band aid their ills with clothes and meals. We needed to change lives to save lives.

We were once again pushed into a new direction but were unsure of where or how. A few weeks later I received a letter from Flint Community Schools. They were consolidating their neighborhood schools. The school board decided to close thirteen schools. They closed all their leased buildings.

The school district had been leasing our school for several years. For the church community it created an issue. What do we do with an empty forty-two thousand square foot building? How do we cope with losing $84,000 in income? Our church was the largest in Genesee county seating over one thousand people but our community was small. How long could we exist in the face of this loss.

I called parishioners together for a town hall meeting. The challenge before us - what should we do with this building? The suggestions were two: open a charter school or do something for women and children. Those present unanimously chose to do something for women and children with the caveat that Sr. Carol and I do it. A lot of these men and women had been on the streets with us and they were well aware of the need.

In June the Flint Community Schools started moving out. We did a walk through the building to see in what condition the facility was left. The carpeting needed replacing, walls needed painting and patching. Roof leaks had stained ceiling tiles and lighting needed attention. The parish could not afford to pay for the refurbishing.

Sr. Carol and I were stymied by the challenge of fixing a 24 classroom building with a gym. We concluded that if this was what God wanted to do it was up to God to show the way. He planted these dreams in our minds; we agreed to do His will and that it would require Him to make a way.

A friend of ours, Madeline, a hairdresser who kept us looking good, asked us what we were going to do with the school building. We began to share our dreams and the new mission we had in mind for the women in Flint. We told her what obstacles we were facing with the building. "I want to be part of this ministry somehow," she said.

A couple of days later she dropped by and took a tour of the building. "Are you going to use the entire facility?" she asked. We told her "no". We had selected a six classroom area in the middle of the building to begin our planning. While showing her the area Madeline said, "The carpet is awful. You don't want women coming into what they already settle for in their homes." We agreed but had no financial assets to do anything about it.

Madeline knew a lot of people. Unbeknown to us she put the touch on a carpet salesman she knew. She showed up one day and said, "If you can get the old carpet up and out of here, Sid would put down new. He will be over in a few days to measure."

We asked the parish for some volunteers and called on friends from other parishes. We have never stripped a floor of carpeting and had no idea how much work that would be. Our volunteers found muscles they hadn't used in a long time. Someone brought in a tool that takes up carpeting and the work moved faster.

Once the carpet was up and out another unanticipated job cropped up. The glue had to be sanded off the concrete floor! One of the men suggested we rent a floor sander. Great idea! Great big dusty mess! Once finished and floors were mopped clean of glue dust we had one more task to accomplish before carpeting was laid. Paint and patch walls!

These stalwart volunteers were working in the peak summer heat. The building was not air conditioned. These men and women were heroic to hang in there. We had to beg for paint, brushes, etc. A Benson's paint store downtown gave us paint. We got a lot "rejected" paint from Home Depot. One of our volunteers was a painter and got his supplier to donate paint, brushes and rollers. Each room was a different color. We had completed six classrooms, two restrooms, the entrance and hallway.

Sid brought carpet samples for color selection. He ordered what we needed and the carpet layers completed the job. The newly painted rooms with fresh carpeting changed the old school into a beautiful building. One of the neighborhood kids came in to look around and said to me, "Wow, how come it didn't look like this when we came here to school? This is cool."

A week later I called Sid, "Where's the bill for all of this?" "It's all taken care of," he said. I thanked him profusely but he told he had nothing to do with it, Madeline paid the bill. This was the beginning of a long line of wonderful friends and donors that God sent to let us know He was serious about what He wanted us to do.

Chapter Five
"If You Build It..."

We did not abandon the street ministry nor did we close our food pantry. We just added the St. Luke N.E.W. Life Center (North End Women's), a name suggested by Jan, a friend and volunteer.

The north end, the most underserved area of Flint, marks our location. Part of it was famous, the Civic Park area, established by GM as the first subdivision in America, a housing development built for its employees. It was a beautiful part of Flint. Most of our parishioners raised their families here and built wonderful memories of better times.

Their homes have deteriorated, some only have a chimney marking were the house was built. Others have been demolished in attempts to eradicate blight while others wait for the wrecking ball. Jungles of overgrowth have replaced the tailored lawns and landscaping; they have become harbingers for dog packs, raccoons, rats, and drug trafficking. Besides animal predators, there are human ones, too.

It didn't look too bad when I went to St. Luke in1994. When you're in the midst of a changing neighborhood you don't see it happening until all of a sudden the changes can't be ignored any longer. Twenty-one years later it becomes a war zone; gunfire becomes commonplace. At night people stay indoors and when they hear gunfire they grab their children and hit the floor. Too many drive-by shootings have killed family members and friends. They don't want to be another tragic statistic.

The area around St. Luke is one of the most dangerous in Flint. One Sunday night two people were shot and killed in our parking lot because of a drug deal gone bad. It was on the morning news. When we got to work there was no evidence that anything had even happened. How come we can clean up the violence better than we can prevent it?

This is where the N.E.W. Life Center becomes a key player. While we were readying the building women would stop by and ask what we were going to do here. We told them this would be a women's center for them to come for a variety of things, similar to a senior center only much, much more. We asked if they would be interested in something like that.

Since we were reluctant to presume what their needs might be, we went to our food pantry and invited the long term clients to come to a meeting. Forty-two women showed up for it. We asked them what they needed from a center for them. Their answers were: "We need a safe place to go; we need to grow in self-esteem; and we need more education." We did some brainstorming with a small group of twelve women who seemed more motivated than others. We decided to create a three-year plan of life change. We chose three years because life change takes time. Together we plotted out the first year of offerings.

Self-esteem building was definitely one of the core classes. Sr. Carol taught sewing so she could help them make curtains for their homes. They loved sewing. Eventually they all learned to make quilts. They discovered they had real talents on which they could build their self-esteem. We had time for conversations that became group counseling sessions. They were able to encourage one another through the tough times in their lives. Parenting classes helped them immensely.

Each year new components were added like computer classes. When we opened we had a computer room set up. One night we were broken into and every computer and printer was taken. It took a while to set up another one but God sent us more computers than we could use. So when the women became familiar with the computer we gave them one for home. They could practice at home and the kids could use them for homework. By the end of the third year we had a twenty-three component program in place.

Another issue for the women was a lack of education. Seventy-five percent did not graduate from high school, some due to learning disabilities, others dropped out to take care of their babies, or they were told they were too stupid to learn. The need for an education was huge in every new group we started. We opened a literacy center. Thanks to the Adrian Dominican Sisters we are now part of the Dominican Rea Literacy Centers.

When all is said and done the core need was someone to care whether they lived or died. A listening ear was the best gift we could give them. Every woman who came to the center knew we cared. Twelve women came and then more and more followed. We never advertised, never needed to; the women themselves passed the word around.

Chapter Six
We Need to Do More

The first group of women who came to the center was able to get jobs or go on to college or learn a trade. The second group was not as fortunate. Employment opportunities had been declining as GM began moving Flint jobs elsewhere. It began as a trickle and soon became a tsunami. Outsourcing became the name of the game and before long Buick City was gone. Eighty thousand employees dropped to seven thousand, five hundred by 2013. The population, once at 200,000 declined to 99,700. The second largest city in Michigan now ranks seventh. Workers left the city in droves, even leaving the state to find employment.

The city lost a huge tax base. Small manufacturing companies supplying parts for the automotive industry also closed their doors. What would this mean for our women? Would we need to change our mission? Our mission to help women become self- sustainable providers for their families was seriously at risk. We prayed, we talked, we decided that we needed to create jobs at the center. We had to do more.

All our women in the course of the three-year program learned to sew; sewing was the way to go. We created a small business making scrubs. There were four hospitals at that time with numerous people needing scrubs. We had four women working part time. Sr. Carol trained the ladies in making scrubs. They sewed, ripped out, and re-sewed until they had mastered the work.

Word got around and we began to sell to doctors' offices, individuals, even one hospital ordered our scrubs for their patients in their psyche unit. We were small enough we could customize for those with special needs. We made scrubs up to size 6x. We accommodated those who needed one size for the top and a different size for bottoms.

One day on a conference call a gentleman asked Sr. Carol, "I was just in the hospital. Can't you do something about those gowns? The exposure is terrible." That was a great idea. Create hospital gowns that don't open down the back. We did. We made them for ambulatory patients, bed ridden patients, as well as gowns needing pockets for monitors and wires.

We needed more seamstresses but had no money to hire any. Can four women handle the additional challenge? "Okay, God, this whole ministry is your design. If we are to do this, help us out."

Once again we got a call from New Paths. "We received a grant to train felons for employment possibilities. Would you like some women to train for your sewing business? We will pay their salary. It's one way we can support you for helping us." "Yes, absolutely," was our response.

Five women came for training and gave us a total of nine women in the sewing business. We hired them when the grant was no longer available. By then we were selling scrubs and gowns and could keep them employed with us.

The women had to take a giant leap of faith to make this business work. Their main fear was losing state assistance. As soon as they get their first paycheck they lose all or part of their assistance. They lose food stamps or at least get a reduction of support. They could lose their housing assistance and/or SSI. They had expressed these concerns and we weighed the pros and cons with them.

When we handed them their first paycheck we weren't sure how they would react. We expected the worst and got the best. There was dancing and check waving accompanied by "We did it. A real paycheck! We made it, didn't we?" Food stamps were cut but employees automatically were eligible for food from our food pantry.

Having a business made it necessary for us to have a receptionist. KK, yes it is a real nickname for her, was our first choice. She and her two sisters had graduated from the program. She tried sewing but was a little too ADD to sit at a sewing machine. They were all hired part time.

KK's mother died when she was young. She has a memory of seeing a man slip something into her drink. An ambulance took her mother away and she never saw her again.

She and her sisters lived with their grandmother. Then grandma got sick and was left paralyzed on one side, most likely because of a stroke. KK dropped out of school in the eleventh grade to take care of her grandmother. When she died it was a huge blow. "She was the only mother I had really ever known."

KK got pregnant at 18, living with an abusive and controlling man. Desperate to get out of the situation, when he went to work, she and her baby escaped through a window. She never looked back.

When we met KK she was on disability and raising a second female child. KK has heart issues and it complicated her life. There wasn't enough money to make ends meet. There was a three-year waiting list for housing assistance. Food stamps didn't stretch far enough and she became a regular at our food pantry.

Since finishing the program KK stated, "I'll never be in the system again. The sisters taught me to be self-sufficient, and once I learned I could stand on my own, I got off disability and came to work at the N.E.W. Life Center.

Before I got my GED, I saw myself as the woman who answers phones. Once I earned my GED, I gave myself permission to say, 'Yep. I'm the Receptionist now!'" (Faith Magazine, June 2015)

We had to keep pushing her to get this GED done. We told her that once she had it she'd be eligible for a pay raise. When she finally accepted calling herself the "Receptionist" her first question to us was, "Do I get a raise now?" She did!

Chapter Seven
And Along Came Steve

In 2008 the Diocese merged four parishes together: Sacred Heart, St. Agnes, St. John Vianney and St. Luke. Three parishes in the north end of Flint were merged with St. John Vianney. It is a very difficult thing for parishes to be closed. It's genuinely the death of life together for close-knit small communities. The day we closed the church doors at St. Luke, the two ushers given that responsibility could not keep back the tears. They were charter members who hauled the bricks, ran the bingos, ushered, did repairs, and were always there for church events. In their later years they served at funeral liturgies and luncheons. They knew where every wire and plumbing pipe was located. They could fix just about anything.

These men and women worked at GM, Buick, Chevy, A.C. Spark Plug. The church was the center of their social life. Neighbors became extended families who met weekly at Mass. St. Luke was originally built to handle the overflow of GM Catholics between St. Agnes and St. John Vianney. With a 1,028 seating capacity, there was standing room only for holidays like Christmas and Easter. These families truly worked together and prayed together. And with the clank of the closing door it was over.

The three parishes that were designated to merge with St. John Vianney suffered some losses in membership. We lost about thirty percent of our people overall. Some just stopped going to church; others joined more evangelical churches; others are still roaming Catholics trying to find a parish to call home.

All of our churches were committed to caring for our neighbors. We had programs for kids, food pantries, and other services. By the time the closures came, St. Luke had completely filled the 42 thousand square foot school building with outreach services. The Bishop gave us the school building and the convent in order not to interrupt our outreach. Sacred Heart and St. Agnes had no space to continue their services. The three closed churches were up for sale. St. Luke and St. Agnes were purchased and a while later Sacred Heart was bulldozed.

The poor were still there. They still needed assistance. We still needed the Catholic presence in the entire north end. After two years we decided to merge food pantry activity and St. Luke became the site of distribution for all four parishes. We initially serviced a couple of hundred people per month. We now serve over 2,500 with groceries and we serve three meals per week.

Fr. Tom Firestone, pastor of St. John Vianney, accepted us as the outreach program for the parish. He would bring people over for tours and conversations about what we did. One such person was a young man he hired as development director. He envisioned that this young man could be of service to do development for us, too. Thus Steve came into the N.E.W. Life Center, a guy with a unique laugh and a huge heart. We didn't really know how lucky we were. He's taken us on a mind-bending journey from services and programs to dreams of changing Flint, re-inventing Flint, and inviting the "throw-a-ways" of Flint to do it. I was told by the men for whom we eventually started a job preparation program that this northwest quadrant of the city is known as the "throw-a-way zone."

Steve connected us with CEOs from major companies (Diplomat, Dr. Nita Kulkarni, Landaal Packaging, and Shaltz Automation) to help guide us in growing our business. He brought hospital CEOs to the table as well as other men and women who wanted to help support our mission. Dr. Nita, an OBGYN, buys our hospital gowns and sells them to her patients to bring to exams and to the hospital for delivery. The women love them in the hospital because they can nurse their babies and maintain their sense of modesty. RMI (Regional Medical Imaging) uses several designs for diagnostic tests in all five offices.

Steve also found us a funding source, the MEDC (Michigan Economic Development Corporation) that brought us into a relationship with Governor Snyder who so much loved what we were doing that he invited us to his state of the state talk and highlighted what we were accomplishing in Flint. His plan for funding was to give financial incentives to companies to hire structurally unemployable residents. Because of this assistance we were able to employ the women full time. Steve's strong belief was that the best way to end the violence was with a job; Flint's crime rate decreased by thirty percent.

Steve's investment in the center has created bonds of friendship with us and our employees that will be unending. He was at our first graduation ceremony and was so moved by their stories and accomplishments that he had to wipe away some tears. It cemented his commitment to the Center.

All the women love and appreciate who he is and what he continues to do for them. One day when he dropped by to say "Hi," to the women, Miss Jessie shared with him that in her prayers God told her Steve was going to do great things in this world. She was so right - he is doing just that.

Chapter Eight
Miss Jessie

In her own right, Miss Jessie is also doing great things. But it hadn't always been that way. Jessie came to the center encouraged by her daughters who had come before her. They kept at her until she decided one day to check it out. She came and stayed.

Jessie grew up on a farm in Louisiana. On the farm she remembers making clothes from flour bags and thinking that she and her siblings looked pretty stylish. At seven years old she came to Flint to live with her sister.

She felt loved and cared for by her sister and her husband. She got store bought clothes ("They dressed me real nice.") and she went to school. They made her feel special.

She and her sister went home for Christmas. While there Jessie realized how difficult it was to provide for their eight children. She continued to live with her sister. She had stability for a while.

At fifteen her dad sent for her. They needed her on the farm. She was taught to drive the tractor and make furrows for planting. School and work in the fields was the substance of each day. Her education ended in the eleventh grade because she got pregnant. Her dad told her to get out of his house because he couldn't feed another mouth.

She and the boy married. It proved to be a loveless marriage. He was violent. He beat her on a regular basis. She stayed in the marriage because she couldn't survive alone. They had five children but he was no help with them at all. He was unemployed which made things worse.

He rejected the fifth child which she named after him; he said it wasn't his. One day Jessie went to her mom's to pick up a few things and left the baby home with her husband. Returning home she found her eight month old baby lying on the bed. He was dead.

Jessie called her sister and she came to Louisiana and brought the entire family, including the husband, to Flint. He didn't stay too long because it was so cold. He went to New Orleans becoming a loan shark. He must have dealt with the wrong people. He was found dead in the river, stabbed seven times.

Some time passed and Jessie became acquainted with another man. He was abusive and devious. She tried to get rid of him but to no avail. She thought if she married him he'd change. He got more abusive. Neighbors were always calling the police because the beatings were so severe. Eventually the police removed him from the home.

He started stalking her. If he showed up in the parking lot where she was working, she wouldn't leave. Her place of employment had a women's locker room. She spent several nights sleeping on the wooden benches. She often used wipes to clean herself because she was too scared to go home.

On weekends Jessie cooked meals for the kids to eat if she didn't make it home. Sometimes she was trapped in the house because he would keep driving by and shoot it up. There are still bullet holes in the garage door. On one occasion she had to risk going out because one of her sons got into trouble and the police called her to pick him up at the juvenile facility.

Jessie was extremely frightened because her husband had just driven by her house. She pulled out of the garage and drove in the opposite direction. He must have seen her in his rear view window. She hadn't driven too far when he pulled up next to her a traffic light. "All I saw was the shot gun he had pointing at my face. I hit the gas but he shot anyway and blew out the back window. The bullet came through my seat and I still have it in my back." He didn't go to jail for long but the abuse stopped. Jessie was free.

Jessie ended up on medical and mental disability. A heavy shroud of depression covered her. Food became her hiding place and comfort. Her weight increased to 450 pounds. Her daughters had been coming to the N.E.W. Life center. They told her, "Mama, you should go up there; it's nice."

One day she decided to go to the Center. "I was sitting with Sister Judy and she said, 'Miss Jessie, is there anything I can do for you? Anything that you need?" Miss Jessie just broke down and started crying. "I'm not used to people doing things for me and the way she asked I felt I could tell she meant it." (Faith Magazine, March 2015.)

"Sister asked me, 'Do I want to work? All you need to do is sew a straight line.'" She said she did and Sister Carol took Jessie under her wing and taught her to sew. She is one of our best sewers and does most of the sewing of fabric. She's always there, always on time. Since she came to the center she has lost 270 pounds; she annually walks 5K in the Crim Race. It's a prestigious race that brings in 30,000 participants from all over the country and overseas.

The church to which she belongs has recognized the value of her wisdom and prayerfulness so the pastor asked her to join the ranks of mother. Mothers are there to help younger women to find their way in faith and life.

"The Sisters have played a beautiful role in my life. They have seen me grow and I have seen myself grow in their presence. They let you know you are somebody. I could see something in them. They are free hearted and they're always here for me."

Jessie came to believe that all the trials she had struggled through were for a reason; it was to become a servant of the Lord. "The Lord brought me through so I could give you a blessing... I am a blessing from God, and I've been a blessing all along. Now I can just see it."

Chapter Nine
Day by Day

The daily work of the Center is always full of unknowns. Each day presents its own challenges and surprises. No two days are the same. The one daily thing we are sure of is that we will be tired at the end of the day.

Our day starts before 9 a.m. preparing for the known activities, getting rooms ready for classes or meetings. Employees find their way to the work of the day. Inevitably we are bombarded with questions. There are days when we have to say, "Can you wait until I at least get my coat off?" The issues can vary from "Sr. Carol, there's no toilet paper in the men's bathroom" to the news of a shooting over night that killed a relative of an employee; or "Sr. Judy, we don't have enough beef to give out in the food pantry." "Do we have extra chicken?" I ask. "Yes, we have lots of chicken." "Then give out extra chicken."

People are constantly in and out of our building. They may be dropping off donations of clothes, small and large appliances or furniture. Others come for a tour to see how they might volunteer or financially support the works of the Center. Mostly they come seeking help.

Besides our regular programs we serve three meals per week, distribute groceries twice per week from our Food Pantry, operate a clothes closet and give away the furniture and appliances. Yes, there is Goodwill, Salvation Army, and the St. Vincent De Paul Society but those agencies sell their items. Most of the clients who come to us do not have money or transportation to get to those organizations.

Oftentimes a case worker will come with their client seeking help after a fire when the family has lost everything. A VA worker comes with a homeless Veteran looking for food and a job. A distraught woman comes seeking counsel.

On food distribution days the recipients call in for appointments to pick up their food. Each person can come once per month for food. Food packages are set up for the number of people in the family because "one size order fits all" does not fit all. We will take walk-ins if the number of orders called in is 100 or less.

On a day when we were over the top with clients, a grandmother raising grandchildren was sent to me for approval of assistance. She looked terrible and told me she was just discharged from the hospital. She had some stomach surgery. She lifted her shirt to show me her incision. I have never in my life seen such an ugly stapling job. It looked like a child used a stapler for the first time in its life. She was in a lot of pain. She said the grandchildren were at home and she needed food for them. Of course, we gave her food but I was angered by what I saw. If I had that surgery I know my incision site would be done straight with evenly placed staples, but then I have an insurance card.

Another time a gentleman came through with no appointment. He related that he just got back from Texas with four grandchildren and did not have enough food to feed all of them. Their mother was killed in a car accident and he was going to have custody of the children. I took him to the sign-in table and explained the circumstances. While sitting with him and the volunteer servicing him, he started to cry and said, "This was my only daughter. It hurts so bad." The volunteer began crying; she too had lost a child. She understood his pain fully and was able to lend support. A week later he came again with a special request. One of the newly arrived children had her seventh birthday and he was wondering if we had a birthday cake. The previous day we received two pallets of sweets from the Food Bank. There just happened to be a large pink frosted birthday cake among the sweets. I wish you could have seen the huge smile on his face when he accepted that cake.

A real shocker that hit all of us one day was the death of one of our employees. She was young and appeared to be very healthy. She went to emergency with an unbearable headache. They sent her home with some pain killers. Her next trip to the hospital was by ambulance. She had a double stroke, one on each side of her head. She was sent to Ann Arbor U of M Hospital. They were not able to save her life. She left a husband and three children behind. She was a beautiful young lady, very artistic. She brought in a picture she had drawn of her baby. It was worthy of a high place in an art gallery. She was a wonderful sewer and created huggable cats and other sewing projects and had a great future ahead of her. We all miss her very much.

Many are the reasons people walk through our doors. Many are seeking help for utility bills when they get a shut off notice. Flint has unthinkable water rates that the poor cannot afford. If they own their home but haven't the money to pay the water bill a lien is placed on the home.

One of my volunteers lives on minimal social security and her monthly water bills are atrocious. Every month she would get a shut off notice. She figured if she paid just what was wanted to prevent the shut off that was all she paid. The next month's bill would come with the water charge and another $90 of extra fees.

She is only one of the 63% of the population who can't pay water bills. We do not have funding for paying bills for our clients. It's really hard to keep saying "Sorry we can't help you." It really hurts to not be able to cover needs for heat, lights, and water.

Recently Flint water was declared dangerous to drink for those with health issues and could eventually cause cancer. Warnings for those with kidney disease, liver disease, and other organs were also given. At the Center, most of the people we serve have those health issues. We will not serve Flint water. We are now buying water cooler size bottles to cook with and to drink. I have kidney disease and can relate to the fears our clients have. Just last week we got another water testing report. There are still unresolved issues and it is still not safe.

Everyone in Flint has a story of hardship of some kind. How the poor manage to survive humbles us. We are amazed at their courage to face each day knowing there's not enough food some days to feed the kids and having to go to several food pantries to provide what food stamps can't. Yet they come to us for food and when we ask how they are the response is always "Blessed" or "Blessed like you."

At day's end our reflections remind us that Jesus spent most of his time with the poor. He loved their openness to his word. They learned to trust in him and he worked miracles for them. Their faith was strong. So is the faith of those we meet every day. Before we close our eyes to sleep, we thank God for the privilege of our ministry among his poor.

"Day by day, oh dear Lord three things we pray; to see thee more clearly, love thee more dearly, follow thee more nearly..."

Chapter Ten
Running in Cement Shoes

Just imagine that you signed up to run a ten-mile race but you had to wear cement shoes instead of running shoes. Sound impossible? Sometimes when people decide to change their lives. Accomplishing this can seem as impossible as wearing cement shoes.

This describes one of our younger women who came to us from New Paths. New Paths is a residential program for men and women within 90-days of reentry into society from jail or prison. We do some of their programming for the women.

In one group that came to us was a young woman in her early twenties. She arrived with an incorrigible attitude and a huge chip on her shoulder. God sent her to us to test the limits of our patience and she did.

There were several times we called New Paths and told them not to send her back to us. Yet every time the van came Rachel was on it. We didn't learn much about her in the classes. She was closed except to criticize or give smart answers to make the ladies laugh.

Just before the doors of freedom opened for her she let us know we wouldn't see her again. I thought that was a good idea but in the back of my mind I had an inkling we would see her.

It was quite a while later that she walked into our lives again. She came looking for help. It was then we began to hear her story.

Rachel was born in Flint, MI, into a family that was drug addicted. The drug of choice was heroine. Her mother used heroine throughout her pregnancy and she was born addicted. Child Protective Services (CPS) took custody of her for two years and then she was given back to her mother.

Their home was a drug house catering to dealers and buyers. As she got older she began to understand the guy crumpled motionless on the bathroom floor had overdosed and was dead. The frequency of these events became commonplace and she became immune to it.

She also became immune to being passed around to these visitors and became numb to the abuse. She was hardened to life itself, especially when her grandmother died of an overdose on the floor of the living room and the visitors partied around her for three days. They stole anything she had of value to buy more drugs and finally called someone to remove the body.

Rachel went to live with her aunt after that. Her aunt was the only family member that was not addicted. With all that she had experienced, Rachel was more than a handful. She ended up in the girls training center in Adrian, MI, and gave them a run for their money. At age seventeen she had to leave the center and try to make her own way in life.

She went to Ann Arbor and got a job in a pizza parlor. That was ten years ago when Katrina hit New Orleans. Seeing the disaster on TV she decided she wanted to go and help out. There still resided a kindness in her heart that all the bad experiences in her live could not destroy.

She boarded one of the busses taking clean up volunteers to Louisiana. Rachel lived in tents at night and worked clean up all day. She happened to meet a man who took a liking to her. Eventually she got pregnant and they moved to his home in another state. He drank a lot, physically abused her and one day when he came home from work in a drunken stupor set her hair on fire and laughed.

Social services gave her a bus ticket to Flint. She was nine months pregnant; her mother wouldn't house her. Within a short time she went into labor. She called the father of the child and he came to be with her. When the child was born the baby was taken by CPS because of what the father did to Rachel. He left town and she lost her baby.

Trying to survive on the streets she met some people who led her into the criminal justice system. They broke into a house to find money and things to hock. As the police were arriving the others left out the back door. She got scared and ran out the front door into the police. Judged guilty of second degree home invasion Rachel was sentenced to jail.

Rachel was out of New Paths this time and the help she needed was to get her child back from CPS. She needed a job and a residence. Could we help her with a job? "You want a job here? With us?" I asked. "You want a job here? With us?" I asked a second time. "Yes and I promise I won't act like I did when I was here before. I don't have anyone else to turn to. Please, I'll do anything."

Sr. Carol and I gave her a second chance. She began working with us in the food pantry. It became evident that she had skills that could take her places. She could organize everything but filing; she was never taught that. However, she had an empathetic response to the needs of our clients.

She began setting up a number system for the men to make sure the food went out in numeric order. She learned how to do intake. She quickly picked up all the functions of running the food pantry.

Rachel went to parenting classes and tried to take some college classes at Mott Community College. She carried a 4.0 in the couple of classes she took. She was living with a man she met at New Paths and he helped her study, taught her to take notes, etc. She did all the right things and her daughter was returned to her.

Rachel became pregnant and gave birth to another little girl and two years later another little girl was born. Rachel is a good mother; life just interferes and brings setbacks. She experienced a meltdown.

We learned that Rachel had mental issues and was diagnosed as bi-polar with psychotic issues. We had experiences with her disabilities and suggested she seek help. That began a long series of drug trials that made her worse. She was hospitalized a few times and the cycle continued and somehow the Rachel with the 4.0 disappeared figuratively and actually.

She began smoking weed instead of taking medications. She dropped out of sight and would not return phone calls. We were concerned but knew that one day she would come through those doors again. Rachel needed someone consistent and stable in her life. We would be there and she knew it.

Today her children are not with her. She will need to work once again to get them back and I believe this will happen. I also believe this will be her last fight to gain success. Rachel has found God in her life and weed is gone. God found her in her home in the emptiness and silence of being alone. She had no heat, no electricity, and only junk food. But she had herself and God and it made a huge difference in her life.

It was just two weeks ago that I sat in St. Rita's Church in Clark Lake, MI, and listened with awe as she told her story to the congregations at three Masses. We were very proud of her that through her witness others may find hope and some told they did.

She is a strong advocate for the N.E.W Life Center and her story is compelling. She gets a lot of support from those who hear her. I'm sure some day she will answer God's call to open a home for women who have had some of her experiences. She will be a blessing to them.

Rachel, it's time for you to remove your cement shoes and run the race uninhibited. Run like the wind, free in mind and heart, and let God raise you up on eagle's wings.

Chapter Eleven
Who is Stormy Kromer?

Some of you may know him quite well or at least know of the products made and sold in his name. Stormy is no longer with us but his legacy is.

As the story goes; Stormy Kromer was a minor league baseball player. He came from a town in Michigan's Upper Peninsula (U.P.). He hails from Ironwood, located at the farthest point west in the U.P. and close to Lake Superior where the winds blow strong and the snow piles up in winter. He earned his name "Stormy" from his behavior on the baseball field.

Ironwood was known for mining and they also had a ski flying structure where people could practice for Olympic Games.

When Stormy left baseball he became a train engineer. He used to wear baseball caps but every time he stuck his head out the engine window for a glance at the tracks ahead, his hat would get blown off his head. In the winter that made it very cold when he lost his hat.

He asked his wife who was a seamstress to figure out a way that he could keep his hat on his head and keep him warm. Do you remember wearing a winter hat with a bill and ear flaps? Stormy Kromer's wife designed it.

Engineers and miners were asking for hats. It was cold in the mines too and miners wanted them. The requests kept coming in so fast that Mrs. Kromer had to hire six women to meet the demand and the SK Brand was born.

Today these hats and other clothing items are still in production in Ironwood, MI. All are made from wool: hats, mittens, vests and shirts and guaranteed for life.

Okay - so what does that have to do with our story? Bob Jacquart, the current owner, was in Lansing for a meeting with the Michigan Economic Development Corporation (MEDC). In a conversation with the MEDC director Bob stated that he doesn't have enough women or men to sew their products and he would have to look out of state for employees. Bob was informed about the N.E.W. Life Center and he wasted no time in contacting us.

We were struggling trying to acquire sewing jobs and were on our way to a lay off when we received Bob's call. What an exciting opportunity put before us! He came to the Center and was pleased by what he saw.

A few weeks after his visit we were planning a trip to Ironwood to train our women to sew on different machines and test our ability to do the work he needed done. This trip would be exciting for the women since only a couple had been out of the state in their life time.

We needed a vehicle to get eight of us to Ironwood. So we contacted a friend of ours, Andy Suski, who owns a car dealership. I told him what we were doing and asked if we could rent a van for the trip. He said, "No, you can't rent one, I'll give you one for the trip." As luck would have it there was no van available so two salesmen, Fred and Jason gave us their SUVs for the trip.

We left the Center on Monday at 7:30 am in the rain. A concern we had was about crossing the Mackinac Bridge. This five mile span across the Straits of Mackinac often creates issues for some drivers. It is anxiety but our anxious driver put her ear buds in, listened to music, and kept her eyes closed. She made it.

The weather was clear in the U.P. The highlight of the trip to Ironwood occurred when a black bear cub scooted across the road in front of our car. We used to go to the dump in Newberry to see bears but years ago they fenced in the dump. This sighting was much more exciting than the dump.

The trip took about twelve hours but there is a time change and we arrived around 6:30 pm at the motel in Ironwood. We ate, unloaded the car, and called it a day. The women would need to be to work at 7:00 am.

I loved going camping in the U.P. because it was always cool and beautiful. Rarely does the temperature get uncomfortable, unlike the heat and humidity of the Lower Peninsula. Flint was hot and humid when we left with an index over 90 degrees. I was extremely disappointed when Ironwood hit 90 degrees! What did they do with the cool air?

On Tuesday morning the ladies went to work at Stormy Kromer's. The women were trained to sew well at the Center. Here they would learn some new machines that would bind, make button holes, and sew on buttons all measured and programmed by computer to increase accuracy and production time.

They were also trained to make two products: woolen mittens and the five pocket vest. The trainers hoped that the women would be able to complete three mittens but our ladies made 12 pair. They passed quality control and went directly to sales. They also did very well at making the vests. Since they practiced using discontinued colors, they were able to bring them home.

We do have to buy the equipment needed and it is now being programmed and tested in Ironwood. Meanwhile we are installing the electrical infra structure needed to run these machines. They should be delivered within a matter of days. Excitement is building and we'll soon be making items for Christmas orders.

So who is Stormy Kromer? He is a legend and we will get to share that legacy. As for us it means we can hire and train more structurally unemployable individuals and help them become self-sufficient providers for their families. Every job we can create will help change the face of Flint and its families. Thank you, Bob Jacquart.

And the journey continues...

Find Out More About St. Luke N.E.W. Life Center

To find out more about St. Luke N.E.W. Life Center, you are invited to visit us online.

Our Website
http://stlukenewlifecenter.com/

Facebook
https://www.facebook.com/StLukeNewLifeCenter

YouTube
https://www.youtube.com/watch?v=VLjSE5L22N0